EPIC GOAT ADULT COLORING BOOK

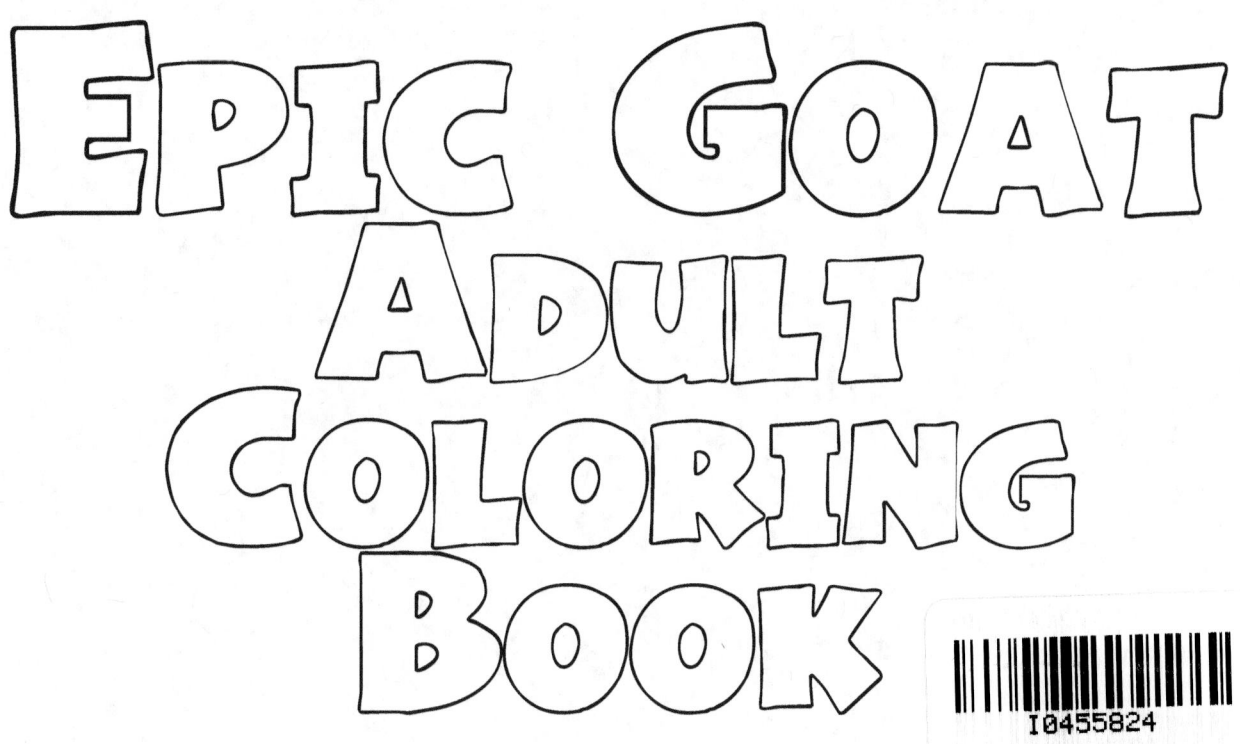

BY SUSAN POTTERFIELDS

Copyright © 2016 Susan Potterfields

All rights reserved.

ISBN: 10: 1535459808
ISBN-13: 978-1535459808

Other Coloring Books By Susan Potterfields

Epic Cat Adult Coloring Book
Epic Dog Adult Coloring Book
Epic Cow Adult Coloring Book
Epic Chicken Adult Coloring Book
Epic Dolphin Adult Coloring Book
Epic Crab Adult Coloring Book
Epic Bear Adult Coloring Book
Epic Turkey Adult Coloring Book
Epic Boar Adult Coloring Book
Epic Sheep Adult Coloring Book
Epic Rabbit Adult Coloring Book
Epic Pig Adult Coloring Book
Epic Fish Adult Coloring Book
Epic Funny Fish Adult Coloring Book
Epic Snack Adult Coloring Book
Epic Deer Adult Coloring Book
And Many More

www.ingramcontent.com/pod-product-compliance
Lightning Source LLC
Chambersburg PA
CBHW052016280526
45793CB00005B/1000